QUESTIONS

and **answers**
from the *Bible*

Questions and Answers from the Bible
Copyright © 1996 Roger Carswell
First edition 1996
Second edition 1998
This edition 2000

ISBN 1 898787 66 2

Ambassador Publications
a division of
Ambassador Productions Ltd.
Providence House
Ardenlee Street,
Belfast,
BT6 8QJ
Northern Ireland
www.ambassador-productions.com

Emerald House
427 Wade Hampton Blvd.
Greenville
SC 29609, USA
www.emeraldhouse.com

QUESTIONS
and **answers**
from the Bible

ROGER CARSWELL

AMBASSADOR
BELFAST ◆ **GREENVILLE**
NORTHERN IRELAND SOUTH CAROLINA

Dedication

To my children,
Emma, Benjamin, Hannah-Marika
and Jonathan.
May their questions long continue and may they always look in the
right place for the answers.

Psalm 119:97-104

CONTENTS

INTRODUCTION

There is a Middle-Eastern proverb which says, *'It is more difficult to ask a good question than it is to give a good answer.'*

In my work as a preacher of the gospel, I am frequently asked questions. Often these are very sincere, though sometimes those who pose them do no want to hear the answers. I have found that whether I am speaking in universities, colleges, schools, youth clubs, churches, radio phone-ins, prisons, men's or women's meetings, or in the open air, the questions are very often the same. In this book you will find many of these basic questions, and briefly the type of answers I give. Perhaps you, too, have asked similar questions. I trust you will find the answers helpful.

The disciple Thomas once asked Jesus, 'Lord ... how can we know the way?' Jesus replied saying, *'I am the way, the truth and the life. No one comes to the Father but by* me.' (John 14:6). Believing and experiencing what Jesus said is the starting point to finding the answers to all life's most vital questions.

I have a friend who talks about the 'R. H. factor'. Is the question a red-herring or a real hindrance in coming to faith? If some of these questions are mere red-herrings to you, I trust that the urgency of finding peace with God will become clear. If some of the questions have been real hindrances, may the brief answers be the catalyst to bring you to the most wonderful moment in life when through Jesus Christ you find peace with God your Maker and Saviour.

WHO
made God?

Nobody expects a dog to buy and read a daily newspaper. This is not because a newspaper cannot be understood, but because it is beyond a dog's understanding. Similarly, God is bigger than anything a mere human can fully comprehend. It is impossible to put God into a laboratory and carry out scientific examinations on Him. God made men and women in His own image. The result is that we have the ability to love, think, reason, hate and to enjoy fellowship. We were created by Him and must not fall into the trap of making God in our own image. We are finite, God is infinite; we are limited, but God is unlimited by time and space; we began and one day our bodies will die, but God has no beginning or end. He was not made by anyone or anything.

Our minds cannot grasp that, just as they cannot understand the fact that there are billions of stars in space, or millions of cells in our bodies. All that **we** know begins and ends, but God had no beginning and will have no end. The Bible says of God, *'The King of kings and Lord of lords, who alone has immortality, dwelling in unapproachable light, whom no man has seen or can see.'* (I Timothy 6:16). If we could fully understand and explain Him, He would not be God.

❧

**The Bible says, 'From everlasting to everlasting,
you are God' ~ Psalm 90:2**

HOW
do you know that there is a God?

Ll that we know about God has not been dreamt up by the fanciful thoughts of theologians or philosophers. God has revealed Himself to us. He has done so in many ways, each being 'a word' which put together forms a complete statement concerning His existence and character. *'In the beginning was the Word, and the Word was with God, and the Word was God.'* (John 1:1). He has shown Himself and therefore spoken through:-

> *Creation* - the material 'word'.
> *Individual conscience* - the unspoken 'word'.
> *Scripture* - the written 'word'
> *Christ* - the living 'word'
> *Circumstances* - the personal 'word'
> *Christian conversation* - the experienced 'word'.

God the Holy Spirit takes hold of these and convinces people of their need to get right with God and find peace through Jesus Christ.

Lord Kelvin, physicist and past president of the Royal Society said, 'If you think strongly enough you will be forced by science to believe in God,' but in answering the question in this book, you will see that the ways listed above in which God has shown Himself have all the hallmarks of being from God. How else can Jesus' resurrection or fulfilled Bible prophecy be explained?

God says, 'You shall seek me and find me, when you search for me with all your heart.' (Jeremiah 29:14).

Astronaut and moon walker, Col. James Irwin said, 'The Creator of this great planet and universe in which it exists is the One who created the laws of science that makes space travel possible. With God in control of our lives, not only can we explore other planets, we hasten hope for this planet.'

WHAT
is God like?

My thoughts about God would not be any more valuable than anyone else's if it were not for the fact that God has shown Himself to us. From God's written Word, the Bible, we read that *'God is a spirit,'* (John 4:24) and so cannot be touched or seen, but *'He has manifested Himself in the flesh.'* I Timothy 3:16.

Therefore, we know that God is not like a genie who appears when an Aladdin's lamp is rubbed, nor a Santa Claus character, nor an old man in the sky! He is not human, and His thoughts are far higher than any of our ideas.

We also know that He is the Creator of all things.

He is all-powerful, all-present, all-knowing. God never changes. He is eternal. God is absolutely holy and pure. He is just and must punish sin, but He is also loving, and in Christ has provided a way whereby we can find forgiveness. God's love and justice met together at the cross. God's love was demonstrated in that He punished Christ for our sin so that we might be declared just in His sight.

It is possible for you to come to know God and for Him, through His Holy Spirit, to live within you and make you His forever.

❧

'God is that, the greater than which cannot be conceived.' ~ Anselm, mediaeval scholar

IS
God green?

G od created heaven and earth and declared all *'very good.'* God gave the fruit of the earth to be food for men and women.

When the first humans sinned, God cursed the earth so that thorns and thistles were to grow and we humans would only live by the sweat of our brows. Death entered into the world, which became a paradise lost.

As tenants of God's earth we are to look after it. There is no excuse for abusing it. The Bible teaches that in war and in peace the land, vegetation and trees are to be cared for and protected. Animals are not to be cruelly treated. Each generation has a responsibility to care for itself and for future generations.

However, people matter more than things. When Jonah was more concerned about a plant withering away than for the people of Nineveh, God spoke saying, 'You have had pity on the plant for which you have not laboured ... and should I not pity Nineveh, that great city ...' Jonah 4:10,11. Principles and trends need to be kept in line with God's priorities and truths.

One day God will destroy this earth with fire, and will make a new heaven and a new earth. Meanwhile, this earth, cursed because of sin, can be a place where God is honoured in the hearts and lives of those who love and serve Him.

☙

Use everything as if it belongs to God. It does. You are His steward. ~ Houston Trier

WHAT
is meant by the Trinity?

There is only one God. That is very clear throughout the Bible. *'Hear, O Israel, the Lord our God is one,'* Deuteronomy 6:4. *'For there is one God and one mediator between God and men, the man Christ Jesus.'* I Timothy 2:5.

In the one Godhead, there is multiple personality. Father, Son and Holy Spirit are equal, and each is God, yet they have distinct works. The Bible says, *'For there are three who bear witness in heaven, the Father, the Word and the Holy Spirit; and these three are one.'* I John 5:7. God is far greater than anything mere humans can ever understand. Nevertheless we have tried to explain and illustrate the triune (three-in-one) God. Some have used H_2O in this way. It is one compound, but can be found in the form of ice, water or vapour. Some have used human beings, being in the image of God, to illustrate Him - each person is one, but comprises of body, soul and spirit. St. Patrick is supposed to have used the three-leaf clover to illustrate the unity and yet three-fold aspect of One God. All these are helpful but inadequate because God is infinite. God has revealed Himself in the Bible as One God, and also as the Father, Son and Holy Spirit are described as having the quality and attributes which only God has. In every great work of God from the creation of the world to the resurrection of Jesus Christ, and to the conversion of an individual, the whole of the Trinity is seen to be at work.

❧

This is such a vital subject that listed here are some Bible verses which teach the Trinity or multiple personality or

deity of the Father, Son and Holy Spirit:- Genesis 1:26 (note the word 'our' and 'us'), Genesis 3:22 (note the word 'us'), Isaiah 9:6-7, Luke 4:18, Matthew 12:28, Matthew 28:18,19 (note the singular word 'name'). Luke 1:35, Luke 3:22, John 15:26, 1 Corinthians 8:6, 2 Corinthians 3:17 and 13:14, 1 Timothy 3:16, Hebrews 9:14, 1 Peter 3:18, 1 John 5:6-7.

Holy, Holy, Holy, Lord God Almighty!
Early in the morning our song shall rise to Thee,
Holy, Holy, Holy, merciful and mighty,
God in Three Persons, Blessed Trinity!

~ Reginald Heber

WHY
bother about God?
I'm alright as I am!

Men and women were made physical beings having a body; social beings with the desire for company; intellectual beings with an ability to reason; emotional beings with a sense of feeling, and spiritual beings - so that we could have a living relationship with our Creator-God.

Sadly, humanity's deliberate disobedience of God has cut us off from Him. The Bible says, 'Your iniquities have separated you from your God; and your sins have hidden His face from you.' (Isaiah 59:2). God is absolutely pure and holy. Let's be honest, we are not. However satisfactory our lives may appear, we are not like the people we were meant to be. Like trying to drive a car when only three cylinders are working, we chug along. Without God, life and death are meaningless. We experience emptiness, but God's desire is that we may enjoy a living, real relationship with Himself.

Even if all appears well now, what happens when you die? I don't know that I could enjoy a journey in an aeroplane, whatever luxuries were given me during the flight, if I knew that there was to be a crash landing at the end. How can I enjoy life if I do not know what will happen when I die? Yet God, through the Lord Jesus has come to this world with the express purpose of dying and rising from the dead, to provide a way for sin to be forgiven, and for people to be brought into a relationship with God which will last through life, death and eternity.

Perhaps God has begun to work in your life already and wants you to trust Him. Are you running away from God or will you receive Him?

Jesus said, 'I have come that they may have life, and that they may have it more abundantly' ~ John 10:10

ISN'T
religion a matter of personal interpretation and sincerity?

However sincere is the person who drinks poison, thinking it is medicine, tragedy is certain. Truth is the key. Deciding what to believe is more like guessing the number of peas in a jar than listing your favourite ten songs in order. One has an absolute truthful answer, the other is subjective. Jesus said, *'I am the way, the truth and the life,'* (John 14:6), therefore don't allow your own feelings to keep you from the objective truth there is in Christ. Faith in Him is not a question of taste but a matter of fact. On the issue of a relationship with God, mistakes have eternal consequences. It is vital, therefore, that personal interpretations are correct.

Though there may be different interpretations concerning some minor teachings of the Bible, the major truths are clear to those who are honest in their dealings with all that it says. This is summarised in the New Testament, *'For I delivered to you first of all that which I also received: that Christ died for our sins according to the Scriptures, and that he was buried, and that He rose again the third day according to the Scriptures ...'* (I Corinthians 15:3,4) and, *'This is a faithful saying and worthy of all acceptance, that Christ Jesus came into the world to save sinners, of whom I am chief.'* (I Timothy 1:15).

Bible teaching should not be abused by private interpretation, or undermined by personal preference simply because what it says is unpalatable. God's Word stands plain to all who will accept it, and God will one day judge all according to what they have done with it.

Be careful of confusion. As one person said: 'I know that you believe that you understand what you think I said, but I'm not sure you realise that what you heard is not what I meant!'

WHAT
is sin?

No other book deals so thoroughly with the subject of sin as the Bible, because no other book deals so thoroughly with its remedy.

Sin is the breaking of God's commandments. It is missing the mark, or falling short of God's requirements. It is a deviation from all that is right - an act of wilful disobedience to God. The Bible pictures sin in different ways:

It is like a burden too heavy for us to carry;
it is like bondage from which we cannot free ourselves;
it is like dirt from which we cannot cleanse ourselves;
it is like a debt we owe God but can never pay;
it is like a disease from which we cannot find a cure.

Yet Jesus said of himself, *'The Son of man has power on earth to forgive sins.'* (Mark 2:10).

Because Christ is the sin-bearer, the burden can be removed;
because He is the Sovereign, the bondage can be broken;
because He is the Saviour, the dirt can be cleansed;
because He is the Surety the debt has been paid;
because he is the soul's Physician, the disease can be cured.

Our lives are often like a pedal-bin whose bin-liner is bursting out and overflowing with all types of rubbish and dirt. The Bible says, *'Now the works of the flesh are evident, which are: adultery, fornication, uncleanness, licentiousness, idolatry, sorcery, hatred, contentions, jealousies, outburst of wrath, self ambitions, dissensions, heresies, envy, murders, drunkenness, revels, and the like; of which I tell you beforehand, just as I also told you in time past, that those who practise such things will not inherit the kingdom of God.'* (Galations 5:19-21).

When God is beginning to speak to an individual he or she begins to feel sinful in the sight of God. After all, He is holy, we are not. God diagnoses us as sinners that He might cure us. He wants to take away guilt and give us new life in the Lord Jesus. God says, *'Come now, and let us reason together, though your sins are like scarlet, they shall be as white as snow; though they are red like crimson, they shall be as wool.'* (Isaiah 1:18).

❧

'Sin as a caterpillar is dangerous, but sin as a butterfly is a thousand times worse. If sin in its ugliest form is dangerous, who can know its unmeasured power and influence when it puts on robes of beauty?'

WHO
decides what is right and wrong anyway?

When people say, 'That's not fair,' or, 'That's not right,' they are in effect saying there is somewhere a standard of right and wrong. We live in a world of absolutes - a builder uses a plumbline, a baker uses weights, a carpenter a ruler, a mathematician consults formulae. But with regard to rules for living, where do we turn? Laws of the land, ideas from leaders, and even standards from organised religion frequently change. God has given to the world unchanging standards, which do not alter with culture or time. As the Creator of all things, He has absolute authority. The best rule is always to follow the Maker's instructions. He loves us and wants the best for us as individuals and nationally.

Christians believe that the law of God is King ('Lex Rex'). He is the ultimate example of genuine love, and we should look to His lordship and law to be free from selfishness. He judges nations and will judge each individual by His standard. God's ten commandments were given to show us what is right and what is wrong. As such, the law is 'our tutor to bring us to Christ,' that men and women might believe and so be declared just in the sight of God.

Summarised, God's ten commandments are:-
1. *You shall have no other gods before Me.*
2. *You shall not make for yourself any carved image... you shall not bow down to them nor serve them ...*
3. *You shall not take the name of the Lord your God in vain ...*
4. *Remember the Sabbath day to keep it holy.*
5. *Honour your father and your mother ...*
6. *You shall not murder.*

7. *You shall not commit adultery.*
8. *You shall not steal.*
9. *You shall not bear false witness ...*
10. *You shall not covet ...*

Jesus went to the heart of the matter by saying that in God's sight, hatred is as bad as murder, lust is adultery in the mind, and that our duty is to love God and love our neighbour as we love ourselves, doing to others as we would like them to do to us.

Most people accept that if we kept God's commands, society would be a 'much better place in which to live'. ·

Do you know God's power to forgive and change you?

∾

The Bible says, 'You shall love the Lord your God with all your heart, with all your soul, with all your strength, and with all your mind, and your neighbour as yourself'
~ Luke 10:27

DO YOU
really believe God made the world?

For centuries people have speculated as to how the world began. 'Where did we come from?' is an intriguing question; but so is, 'Where are we going?' We live in a society which is continually bombarded with the idea that evolution is not just a theory but a fact. The many scientific evidences that actually undermine this theory are not presented to us. Frankly, this is not honest. It takes more faith to believe that there is no cause behind creation than to believe in a Creator. Neither is it right to place the account of creation recorded in the Bible alongside fictional, fanciful stories about the beginnings of the world.

The Bible states as a matter of historical fact that God did make the world. We read, 'In the beginning, God created the heavens and the earth.' (Genesis 1:1). It is reasonable to believe that behind all design there is a Designer, and everything made must have a Maker. The Bible is not unscientific. It does challenge some of the theories which have been widely accepted, but which cannot be tested. It teaches that there is a difference between vegetable life, animal life and human life. Unlike the rest of creation, human beings were made with a spiritual dimension, and are accountable to God.

If God is all-powerful then there is no difficulty in believing that He made the world and knows every detail about all of creation.

God who made something out of nothing is able to make something out of you! Have you experienced this yet?

Here is a thought worth considering: There is about as much chance of this world coming from a big bang as there would be the Encyclopaedia Britannica coming from an explosion in a printing factory.

DO ALL
religions lead to God?

en and women were made to know God deeply and
intimately. When sin severed the link between us and
God, it left an aching God-shaped void within the heart of
each person. Universally religious, human beings strive to fill that
gap. In some countries religion has been brutally suppressed, in others terribly perverted, and in still others it has become a vain attempt
to find God.

Most religions involve people trying to climb up to God. But
He is too great for small humans to reach, and too holy for sinful
humans to contact. Fulfilling the five pillars of Islam, keeping to the
eight-fold path of Buddhism, learning and living by the Hindu teachings, being faithful in attending Mass or confession, working to be
religious, or even seeking to obey the Ten Commandments is not
God's way to draw us to Himself. The Bible says, 'Not by works of
righteousness which we have done, but according to His mercy He
saved us ...' (Titus 3:5).

A drowning man does not want a crowd standing on the sea
shore shouting instructions as to how to swim, especially if those
instructions are contradictory. But if someone were to dive in and
rescue him, that would be different.

God has taken the initiative. Christ Jesus has come into the world
to save sinners, which includes all of us. Whilst other religions try to
point the way to God, Jesus said, 'I am the way the truth and the life.
No one comes to the Father except through me.' (John 14:6). Or as

someone expressed it: 'If all the religions are right then Jesus is right, and if Jesus is right then all the other religions are wrong! Right?' Christ alone was sinless. He alone was big enough to carry and pay for the sin of the world as He died on the cross. He alone can forgive a person and bring him or her to God.

It is possible to visit the graves of the world's greatest religious and political leaders. Christ too, was buried. Three days later, He rose from the dead. There is an empty tomb where Jesus lay. The risen Christ towers above the rest of humanity and surpasses all other leaders. He alone can establish a relationship between us and God. Religion is human kind's sincere desire, but a vain attempt to reach God. Christ is God's only bridge from us to Him. Are you trusting in what you are doing or in what Christ has done to save you?

∽

The Bible says, 'Neither is there salvation in any other, for there is no other name under heaven given among men by which we must be saved' ~ Acts 4:12

HAVEN'T
wars been caused by religion?

The cause of war is basically the sinfulness, greed and weakness of humanity. Some wars were started to bring about peace, others to gain, keep or regain territory, still more to merely advance ego.

Sadly, there have been religious wars. Some religions even believe that it is legitimate to fight if it spreads their cause. That is not so with true Christianity. Jesus said to His followers, 'Turn the other cheek'. He told Peter to put away his sword. Jesus is even called the Prince of peace.

Therefore, if a person fights 'in the name of Jesus', it is like somebody else carrying out a crime in your name when you specifically told that person not to commit it. It would not be fair to blame you, nor is it right to blame Christ for wars. Politics and religion can stir strong feelings, but somebody trusting and obeying Christ will find that He calms aggression and gives a genuine concern and compassion towards all. Jesus commanded Christians to love their enemies and to pray for those who persecute them. He also gives the ability to obey His commands.

❧

If 'Christian nations' were nations of Christians there would be no wars.

DIDN'T

God sanction war in the
Old Testament?

I t is true that there were occasions when God commanded His people to go into battle. He had promised a land for the nation of Israel, and the gaining of that territory at times involved war. There were occasions also when nations had been so wicked and blatantly disobedient to all that was right that, to prevent the spread of such evil (child sacrifices, gross immorality, idolatry and perversion, to name but a few) God ordered the Israelites to go into battle. Eventually, when the people of God started committing the same sins, He used enemy armies to fight against His people and so judge them.

War hastens death and causes great suffering. God did not want this world to be spoiled by sin. Ruin came about when the first man and woman rebelled against God. All of creation was ruined in a moment of time. God's desire is that people should learn war no more, and when Christ comes again to this earth to reign as King, people will beat their swords into ploughs. Until then we should pray, and as much as is possible, work to live peaceably with all people , looking forward to the day when Christ will return. God still judges nations and individuals who persistently fight against Him.

∽

'World peace will come only when all mankind turns wholeheartedly to God in complete humility and voluntary unconditional surrender. Until human nature is changed, we will have war.'
~ Dr. Robert M. Page, Director US Naval Research

WHY
do you believe the Bible?

I'm not sure that I did believe the Bible, until I began to read it. I started at John's Gospel, and as I read I became convinced of its authority and authenticity. It, or rather God, spoke to me through its pages.

The written Word of God is a collection of sixty six books which make up one complete and sufficient volume. Although written over 1550 years ago, by about forty authors from different backgrounds, they have a perfect unity. They each speak of humanity's ruin through sin, and God's remedy through Christ the Saviour. He brought forgiveness, and the Holy Spirit brings new life to those who believe. Imagine today trying to collect the writings of forty authors who have written since 500 AD - what strongly varying ideas they would have! But throughout the Bible there is no contradiction in thought or theme.

The Old Testament part of the Bible looks forward to the coming of Christ; the New Testament part describes His life, death, resurrection and work in the world today. Hundreds of times, in minute detail the Bible prophecies the future. Apart from those concerning the end of the world, these specific predictions have been fulfilled to the letter. For example, crucifixion was devised about 300 BC; but about 700 BC the prophet Isaiah and about 1000 BC, King David describe how Jesus would be slain. They, together with other Old Testament passages, tell us that He would be sold for thirty pieces of silver, have His garments gambled for; die a poor man's death with the wicked people in the prime of His life; be crucified between thieves but be buried in a rich man's tomb; His hands, feet and side would be pierced; His bones would be pulled apart but not a bone in His body would be broken; as He died, He would be bearing the sin of the world on His shoulders, and that He would be buried and rise from the dead.

Only God is able to look into the future and accurately write down in the present what will happen in the future.

The Bible has God's imprint on it. Will you try reading John's Gospel with an open mind and see for yourself?

∽

'I believe the Bible is the best gift God has given to man. All the good from the Saviour of the world is communicated to us through this book' ~ Abraham Lincoln

The Bible says, 'All Scripture is given by inspiration of God, and is profitable for doctrine, for reproof, for correction, for instruction in righteousness' ~ 2 Timothy 3:16

WHY
don't we read about dinosaurs in the Bible?

There are so many creatures and animals, you would hardly expect to read about them all in the Bible. It is not a zoological encyclopaedia! We don't read in the Bible about the dodo either, but that does not mean that there was no such creature, nor that the Bible is untrue. The dodo bird is thought to have become extinct.

However, the Bible does refer to the behemoth (Job 40). The description of it seems remarkably like a dinosaur. We also read in the Bible of large sea creatures.

Like the dodo, the dinosaur has become extinct. It is as straightforward as that.

෴

Then God said, 'Let the earth bring forth the living creature according to its kind: cattle and creeping thing and beast of the earth, each according to its kind'; and it was so. And God made the beast of the earth according to its kind, cattle according to its kind and everything that creeps on the earth according to its kind. And God saw that it was good.
~ Genesis 1:24,25

ISN'T
God different in the Old and New Testaments?

No! God reveals Himself step by step throughout the Bible. We read of His love, and His justice against sin in both Testaments. Of course, there are times in the Old Testament when God gives direct instructions that various people are to be destroyed, but in the New Testament as well, we read of God's righteous anger against those who persist in revelling in wicked ways. God is a just and holy God, and by nature must punish sin. Throughout the whole of the Bible, God's infinite patience is evident, and His love beyond compare. We see the judgment of God against sin, and His love for sinners at the cross. There Jesus took on Himself the wrath of God, paying for our sin, so that if we trust Him, we might find forgiveness and a new life.

❦

God is consistent and unchanging, though different situations call for different emphases. When the two Testaments are read as they were intended, they reveal the same God who is rich in mercy, but will not let sin go unpunished.
~ Josh McDowell

DO YOU
believe everything which is in the Bible?

There are different types of writings in the Bible. For example, there are parables (such as the ones Jesus told); there are symbols (e.g. Jesus said, 'I am the door); there are letters (such as the ones Paul wrote which are in our New Testament); there are history books (e.g. Genesis or Luke's Gospel); there are the words spoken by men and women; we even sometimes read the words of the devil (e.g. in the garden of Eden). However, all Scripture is a true record of what took place. It is 'given by inspiration of God, and is profitable for doctrine, for reproof, for correction, for instruction in righteousness.'

I have found that the very reading of the Bible leads one to start believing it. God speaks to us through His Word, and proves Himself as we read the Scripture for ourselves, instead of simply believing second hand opinions about it. Yes, I believe everything that is written in the Bible.

❧

The best evidence of the Bible's being the Word of God is found between its covers ~ Charles Hodge

CAN'T
you prove anything you want
from the Bible?

There are people who twist and pervert the clear Bible teaching, by taking phrases and verses out of their context. Such practice is dishonest. There are those who peddle their religion with little regard to an honest teaching of the Bible, even sometimes having their own particular adjusted version of the Bible. Obviously, this too, is wrong.

However, if one reads the Bible openly and honestly, the message is very clear - God is the Maker of all things; we have sinned against Him; our own efforts will never be good enough to bring us back into a relationship with God; Christ came into the world to be the Saviour of all who will trust Him; He died paying the punishment for our sin; Christ rose again from the dead; the living Christ empowers people who receive Him into their lives; there is eternity, and God has told us how He will wind up the affairs of this world.

Reading the Bible gives to us the opportunity to discover God's word, will and way. Ignoring the Bible is to neglect the treasure trove which tells us what life is about, and why we are here. Twisting the Scripture to further our own ends is to bring God's rightful anger on ourselves.

༺༻

Preparing for a long trip, a teenage Christian said to his friend, 'I am just about packed. I only have to put in a guidebook, a lamp, a mirror, a microscope, a telescope, a volume of fine poetry, a pile of letters, a book of songs, a sword, a hammer and a set of books I have been studying.'

'But,' his friend objected, 'you'll never get all that in your bag.'

'Oh yes, I will,' came the reply, 'it'll not take that much more space.' He placed his Bible in a corner of the case and closed the lid!

WHY
are there so many versions of the Bible?

The Bible was not written in English! The English language itself is a living and, therefore, changing one. Because the vast majority of the population do not know Hebrew and Greek, the Bible has been translated into our language, to make it accessible to all. Translation from one language to another is never easy, and the quest for accuracy has led new translators to try to modernise and improve previous, greatly blessed works. Some are more accurate than others, some are paraphrases and frankly, some are not very good. The ones most widely used in Britain, by people who really take the Word of God seriously are the Authorised Version (translated in 1611) and the more recent New International Version and New King James Version. Whichever you use, read it each day.

❧

The truth is, that if we are to have a translation at all, we must have periodical re-translation. There is no such thing as translation of a book into another language once and for all, for language is a changing thing.
~ C. S. Lewis in his book 'God in the Dock'

WHAT
are the major themes
of the Bible?

God has spoken to this world through the Bible so that we may come to know four basic things.

First, God wants us to know who He is. It is easy to start making God in our image rather than realising that He is far greater than anything our minds can truly grasp.

Secondly, God wants us to know who we are. We have been created in the image of God and were made and meant to know Him. Sin spoilt that, and leaves us empty knowing that there is something missing. God alone fills the God-shaped gulf in each individual.

Thirdly, God wants us to know what He has done. 'For God so loved the world that He gave His only begotten Son, that who ever believes in Him should not perish but have everlasting life.' (John 3:16). The Old Testament looks forward through poetry, prophecy, and pictures to the coming of Christ, and the New Testament tells us of His life, death, resurrection, exaltation and one-day return. His work and influence are described, detailing God's great rescue mission for men and women.

Fourthly, God wants us to know what we must do. The Bible tells us of God's dealings with His people. It clearly explains the only way whereby people can come to find peace with God.

These are the basic, interwoven themes of the Bible. They deal with life's most crucial issues. When you open the Bible to read, you open the lips of God for Him to speak.

'Behind and beneath the Bible, above and beyond the Bible is the God of the Bible. The Bible is God's written revelation of His will to man. Its central theme is salvation through Jesus Christ' ~ Henrietta C. Mears

HAVEN'T
scientists disproved the Bible?

No! There is absolutely nothing in testable scientific fact that is contrary to what the Bible teaches. Although the Bible is not a scientific text book it is perfectly consistent with all provable scientific teaching.

There are scientists who do not believe the Bible; but that is because they are people who do not believe the Bible;, not because they are scientists!

There are literally thousands of scientists who read, believe and seek to live by the Scripture.

Listen to what some have said:

Samuel F. B. Morse - inventor of the telegraph: *'The nearer I approach the end of my pilgrimage, the clearer is the evidence of the divine origin of the Bible, the grandeur and sublimity of God's remedy for fallen man are more appreciated and the future is illuminated with hope and joy.'*

Michael Faraday - inventor of the electric generator: *'The Bible, and it alone, with nothing added to it nor taken away from it by man, was the sole and sufficient guide for each individual at all times and in all circumstances.'*

Dr. Boris P. Dotsenko - one time head of nuclear physics, Institute of Physics, Kiev: *'Today I know that the Bible is the greatest book of faith, in which the acts of God are recorded for believers. Its final proof will come with the return of our Lord and the establishment of His kingdom'.*

Issac Newton: *'We account the Scriptures of God to be the most sublime philosophy. I find more sure marks of authenticity in the Bible than in any profane history whatsoever'.*

In relation to creation or evolution, it is well to remember that evolution has not and cannot be proved. It is merely theory. A few years ago all the pupils were told that the world is 30 billion years old. Then evolutionists changed their mind saying it was 15 billion years old. That was a big mistake! Supposing it was still another 15 billion younger!

Professor E. Andrews of London University says: *'Christians are not anti-science. We are in agreement with theories such as gravity, electromagnetism, planets revolving round the sun, of light of optics, but we disagree with one because it does not fit into the great picture of truth, it is like a foreign piece in a jigsaw.'*

Let us remember that science has many inadequacies. It does not explain kindness, love, beauty, friendship, fairness, evil and good, where we are going, or the spiritual dimension and human desire to worship,which is found in all people

❧

**This world is not the result of a big bang,
but a master plan!**

ISN'T
the Bible full of contradictions?

I remember being asked this on a late night radio phone-in pro-
gramme. The radio host asked the questioner for an example, but
none could be thought of. As a result the radio interviewer told
him to 'Get off the air and stop wasting our time'. I never spoke a
word in answer to that question!

Since my Christian conversion years ago, I have systematically
read through the Bible many times. I have never found any contradiction in it. It fits together like a complete interlocking jigsaw.

Although a library of books, it is perfectly complete. It has common themes: God is good, life is tough, humanity is sinful, Christ is
the Saviour, faith in Him is God's only way to eternal life.

'An eye for an eye ...' and *'Turn the other cheek'* is often posed
as a contradiction. In fact these two are both valid. *'An eye for an
eye...'* was God's instruction to the nation of Israel who was given
the duty to uphold the law and order and not punish society's wrong-
doers excessively, but with punishment that would fit the crime. That
is still valid for governments today. Speaking to individuals, Jesus
taught that they should not take the law into their own hands. Instead
they should turn the other cheek for Christ's sake, leaving the en-
forcement of law and order to the bodies responsible.

One command is for the nation, the other for individuals. Both
are valid. If one can take verse out of context and setting in which
they were written, of course one can make it appear that there are

contradictions in the Bible, but that is not being fair to God's Word, or to one's own mind.

The message of the Bible is too important to play games with.

∞

'It is not the parts of the Bible I don't understand which trouble me, but the parts I do understand' ~ Mark Twain

WHERE

would you recommend me to start reading the Bible?

God speaks through His word, the Bible. Therefore, it is not easy to single out one passage, but for someone who is beginning to consider the claims of Christ on them as individuals, I would recommend reading one of the four Gospels: Matthew (which looks at Christ as the King), Mark (which emphasises Jesus as a servant), Luke (depicting Christ as the Saviour of the world) and John (which is about Christ, the Son of God). John's Gospel was specifically written to help people come to belief in Christ: *'And truly Jesus did many other things in the presence of the disciples, which are not written in this book; but these are written that you may believe that Jesus is the Christ, the Son of God, and that believing you may have life in His name.'* (John 20:30,31).

✆

Read John's Gospel with an open mind and God will speak to you through His Word.

WHERE
did Cain get his wife?

This is one of those questions passed around in pubs, clubs, school playgrounds and other institutions noted for their great learning! It is asked by people who have not read their Bibles. In asking the question, they are really making a statement, 'I don't believe the Bible and this question is my excuse.'

The Bible clearly answers this question, but I fear that most who ask it will still not take God's Word seriously, because for them the issue is not that they cannot believe, but that they do not want to.

In Genesis chapter five verse four we read that Adam, after begatting Cain and Abel, also had a son called Seth *'and he begat sons and daughters'*. Marriage between such close family relations is unacceptable and problematic to us today. However, Verna Wright, for many years professor of rheumatology at Leeds University says concerning this, *'At the beginning of the human race this was all right. Later, when inter-marriage could be dangerous by increasing the likelihood of disease producing recessive genes manifesting themselves, the Bible itself laid down clear guidelines about this - a remarkable provision when the science of genetics was unknown'*.

In all aspects, the Bible is trustworthy. As it retells historical events, it does so with precision and accuracy. After all, it is God's Word, and He does not make human mistakes.

❧

Boy to R.E. teacher: 'Where did Cain get his wife?'
Teacher: 'I'd tell you if I was Abel!'

WHY
doesn't God stop the trouble?

God made a perfect world where there was no sin or suffering. In an instant of time all was wrecked and ruined in a deliberate act of rebellion which Adam and Eve committed when they disobeyed God. Earth became a 'paradise lost'. Suffering, sin and death became the norm. The first child born, far from regaining paradise, became a murderer.

There is coming a time when God will completely reverse all those ruinous effects. Meanwhile people are born into a world which has been spoiled. Sometimes suffering is the direct result of man's disobedience to God, e.g. the drunkard who destroys his liver through alcohol abuse, or the homosexual who contracts AIDS. At other times it is difficult to understand why one particular person suffers so much whilst another doesn't.

We are, however, all bound up in the bundle of life and often the innocent suffer most. The Bible gives no glib, easy answers; but it does assure us that through it all God knows, loves and cares.

God is the Heavenly Father of all those who trust Him, '... *all things work together for good to those who love God, to those who are called according to His purpose.'* (Romans 8:28). Christians do not always know 'why', but we do know who is in overall control.

Christ fully identified Himself with human suffering. He was forsaken by His friends, neighbours, countrymen and even by His Father, God. He cried, 'My God, my God, why have you forsaken me?' when He was crucified. As He bore the sin of the world His holy Father turned away. Jesus endured such separation so that those who trust Him and believe might experience God's forgiveness and eternal companionship.

He triumphed over sin and death by rising from the dead. One day all who receive Christ into their lives will be able to shake off earth's present darkness and difficulty and enjoy Him forever.

Do you yet know God as a very present help in time of trouble?

Corrie Ten Boom was born in Haarlem, The Netherlands. Towards the end of the Second World War, Corrie, her father and sister were arrested by the Nazis for hiding Jews. Of the three, Corrie alone survived the death camps. After her release from prison, she travelled around the world speaking and writing. Until her death on her 91st birthday in 1983, she was a faithful witness to the love and power of God.

She said, *'Once, when I was in the hospital, I learned something. I was in much pain, and I remembered the pain Jesus suffered for me, for my sins, and for the sins of the whole world. I remembered His love for the world, His love for me, and I received new strength.*

'I also remembered that Jesus went the way to glory through suffering. There is no pit so deep that He is not deeper still.'

❧

The twenty-third Psalm says, 'Yea, though I walk through the valley of the shadow of death, I will fear no evil; for you are with me, your rod and your staff they comfort me.'

SURELY,
when you are dead you are done for?

Yorkshire's song, *'Ilkley Moor Baht'at'* describes a man dying, his body being eaten by worms, then ducks eating the worms, and us eating the ducks, with the conclusion, *'Then we will all have eaten thee ...!'* Change and decay affect all our bodies. However, we are not just bodies.

If somebody says something which 'hurts' you, it is not the body which is hurt but the real, inner you. The soul and spirit, as the Bible calls this, will live forever. *'It is appointed for men to die once, but after this the judgment.'* (Hebrews 9:27).

People say, *'Nobody has ever come back from the dead to tell us,'* but they are wrong. Christ died, then bodily rose again. He is the one who spoke most strikingly about life after death. He spoke of heaven and warned of hell.

Heaven is a place where God is, and where He *'will wipe away every tear; there shall be no more death, nor sorrow, nor crying and there shall be no more pain.'* (Revelation 21:4). It is a place reserved for all who have trusted Christ to cleanse them from the sin which cuts them off from God, in life and in eternity.

∽

'The wicked are like the troubled sea, when it cannot rest ... there is no peace ... to the wicked' ~ The Prophet Isaiah

HOW
could a God of love
send people to Hell?

H ell is a place of awful, eternal and conscious separation from God. Jesus spoke of those who 'will be cast into outer darkness.' He said, *'There will be weeping and gnashing of teeth,'* (Matthew 8:12).

The Bible never speaks of purgatory, or a second chance after death. In fact, Jesus taught that between heaven and hell 'there is a great gulf fixed' so that no person can pass from hell to heaven or indeed from heaven to hell.

God loves us so much He sent Christ to be the escape route from hell to heaven. He is 'not willing that any should perish but that all should come to repentance' (2 Peter 3:9); but for those who refuse to receive Christ as Lord and Saviour, God who is just, has no alternative but to punish sin and the sinner.

It is a fair question to ask, 'Where will you spend eternity?'

The moment you die you will be more alive than ever you were before you died. When people say of you, 'Have you heard? He/she has gone!' Where will you have gone to?

☙

The Bible says, 'And this is the testimony: that God has given us eternal life, and this life is in His Son. He who has the Son has life; He who does not have the Son of God does not have life' ~ I John 5:11,12

DON'T
the good go up (to heaven) and the bad go down (to hell)?

That is a very common idea, but it is absolutely wrong. It feeds human pride and therefore has become widely accepted. But God is too holy and we are too sinful to ever sneak into heaven. On virtually the last page of the Bible we read, 'But there shall by no means enter into it anything that defiles or causes an abomination or a lie, but only those who are written in the Lamb's Book of Life' (Revelation 21:27). No sin at all, not even a little lie is able to enter into God's presence. He is too holy even to look at sin. He can never tolerate it or grow accustomed to its devastating consequences.

Some imagine a judgment to be like a tightrope walker, balancing good with evil deeds. If the good outweighs the evil then all will be well. The Bible teaches differently:-

First, we read the unflattering news that all of us are sinners: 'There is none righteous, no not one ... for all have sinned and fall short of the glory of God.' (Romans 3:10 and 23). Then we read that 'All our righteousnesses are like filthy rags,' (Isaiah 64:6), so we really are in a lost state, except that the Gospel message meets our deepest need because, 'For by grace you have been saved through faith, and that not of yourselves; it is the gift of God, not of works, lest anyone should boast.' (Ephesians 2:8,9). In other words, salvation (God's complete rescue passage) is a gift from God, available to all who will receive it.

That does not mean that it is not good to be good. The world desperately needs more 'good' people.

When a person is right with God he or she will find that the Lord gives a deep desire to be and to do good. That is why Christians have worked for social reform and have given their lives in service as missionaries abroad or at home to help others.

If we love and live for Christ we will find we love and live for others too. However, this is a result of trusting Christ, not as a means of trying to find favour with God.

Heaven is full of bad people ... who have been forgiven. Jesus came into the world for everyone, because He came to seek sinners and we all qualify.

All need to receive Christ and find that He has reserved a place in heaven for them.

∽

A man may go to Heaven
Without health,
Without wealth,
Without fame,
Without a great name,
Without learning,
Without a big earning,
Without culture,
Without beauty,
Without friends,
Without 10,000 other things.
But he can
Never go to heaven
Without Christ.

DO YOU
believe in reincarnation?

No! The eternal God is the one how has told us in His Word, the Bible, *'It is appointed for men to die once, but after this the judgment?'* (Hebrews 9:27). God's knowledge about these things is greater than the fanciful thinking of human beings.

In Luke 16:19-31, Jesus told the story of a rich man, and a poor beggar called Lazarus. Both died. Lazarus, because of his trust in God (that is what his name meant), went to be with God. The rich man who showed his contempt for God by his lack of concern for his neighbour, went to hell. There, in torment, he lifted his eyes to heaven and begged for mercy. The answer came back, *'... between us and you there is a great gulf fixed so that those who want to pass from here to you cannot nor can those from there pass to us.'* Later he was told that if people do not take note of God's Word they will not be persuaded though one rose from the dead.

What a person does with Jesus Christ matters for all eternity. We are not saved by our own works, and our lot in the next life does not depend on us being good enough to achieve high value for the next world. While here on earth, we are either made acceptable in God's sight through the Lord Jesus, or we will be found guilty of rejecting God's remedy for sin, and therefore we will be lost forever.

∽

'Reincarnation is a burden too great to bear' ~ M. Ghandi

WHAT'S
wrong with the occult?

The Bible teaches that there is a devil. He was an angelic being created by God, probably long before our world was made.

Satan wanted God's Throne and led a rebellion against his Creator. He was cast out of heaven, to hell, which was made by God for the devil and his angels. Jesus said, 'I saw Satan fall like lightning from heaven.' (Luke 10:18).

Ever since, Satan's subtle device has been to try to make people imitators of him and turn against God. Satan has power, but not absolute power. He does amazing things, but it is foolish to dabble with anything to do with Satan.

God said to the people of Israel, *'There shall not be found among you anyone who makes his son or his daughter pass through fire, or one who practices witchcraft, or a soothsayer, or one who interprets omens or a sorcerer, or one who conjures spells, or a medium, or a spiritist, or one who calls up the dead, for all who do these things are an abomination to the Lord.'* (Deuteronomy 18:10-12).

Whether it is ouija boards, horoscopes, fortune telling, playing tarot cards or black magic, God forbids it, because He loves us, wants the best for us, and desires to protect us from harm. Innocent 'fun' quickly exposes the person to Satan's influence and power which is real, but wrong. A person can know fullness of joy and peace through knowing God, and does not need to search for the pleasures of sin which last only for a short time.

Christ who resisted Satan's temptations came to destroy the works of the devil, and through His death and resurrection can do that in lives today.

One day the devil will be *'bound ... cast into the bottomless pit'* and eventually *'cast into the lake of fire and brimstone.'* (Revelation 20:2,3 and 10).

Have you experienced complete pardon from and power over sin which comes through Christ's presence in your life?

⬦

'A man beaten by the occult and demons, was ostracised, constantly harmed himself, and resorted to nakedness, shame and mental derangement. Normal human treatment failed to help him. He had a wonderful experience when introduced to the Saviour. His sanity returned, and his decency, composure and joy. From then on he wanted to tell others about Christ, and the deliverance he had found from spiritism.' See Mark chapter five.
~ Trevor Knight, Director of Young Life

WHY
did Jesus die on the cross?

Jesus was born to die. His greatest work was not that of healing the sick, casting out demons, stilling the storm, raising the dead or even teaching the multitudes. It was done in three days. First, Christ died to save us. He was buried. Three days later Christ in triumph rose again.

When the Lord Jesus died on the cross, God laid all my sin on Him. He died as my sin-bearer. The Bible says, *'Who Himself bore our sins in His own body on the tree.'* (I Peter 2:24).

Christ also died and rose to be my Saviour. He is able to forgive my past sin and give me strength to live a new life. He will give me power over sin day by day.

Because of His death and resurrection, Jesus is able to cleanse the past and also control the present and future. He will guide my life and your life as we serve and obey Him in everything. He died, therefore, to be my Saviour and yours. The Bible says, *'For to this end Christ died and rose and lived again that He might be the Lord of both the dead and the living.'* (Romans 14:9).

Jesus died paying for the sins which cut us off from God, keep us out of heaven and would condemn us to hell. If I trust Him for forgiveness, that great barrier between God and me, sin, can be forgiven. I can have a link up to God which will last forever. Christ's death is absolutely vital, because it is the only way I can know God and everlasting life.

Frederick Farrar, in his book, 'The Life of Christ' described crucifixion: 'For indeed a death by crucifixion seems to include all that pain and death can have of horrible and ghastly dizziness, cramps, thirst, starvation, sleeplessness, traumatic fever, tetanus, shame, publicity of shame, long continuance of torment, horror of anticipation, mortification of untended wounds - all intensified just up to the point at which they can be endured at all, but all stopping just short of the point which would give to the sufferer the relief of unconsciousness.

'The unnatural position made every movement painful; the lacerated veins and crushed tendons throbbed with incessant anguish; the wounds, inflamed by exposure, gradually gangrened; the arteries - especially at the head and stomach - became swollen and oppressed with surcharged blood; and while each variety of misery went on gradually increasing, there was added to them the intolerable pang of a burning and raging thirst; and all these physical complications caused an internal excitement and anxiety, which made the prospect of death itself - of death, the unknown enemy, at whose approach man usually shudders most - bear the aspect of a delicious and exquisite release.'

HOW
could Christ die for me when I wasn't yet born?

s a child I remember seeing a small steam engine shunting some goods wagons. One wagon bumped into another, and those into another, and so on, until eventually all the weight of the engine and the wagons went into the guard's van which stood absolutely still taking the impact of all the others on itself.

In a similar way Jesus took the weight of the world's sin upon Himself. Jesus came into the world to go to a cross where He would pay for our sins which would take us all eternity to pay for. He died because He loves us.

When Jesus was on the cross, God who knows all things, took the sin of ordinary people and laid it on Christ.

He died, the just for the unjust that He might bring us to God.

God who is eternal and not bound by time, looked back in time to the beginning, and forward in time to the end, took it all, and laid it on Christ.

> *He knew how wicked we have been;*
> *He knew that God must punish sin;*
> *So out of pity Jesus said,*
> *He'd bear the punishment instead.*

Jesus bore the penalty in our place. His death, therefore, satisfies both God's justice - sin has been punished; and His love - through His mercy we can be forgiven. That does not mean that there is blanket forgiveness for everyone - God offers the free gift of salvation to all who will repent (turn from their sin) and believe (trust in Christ). There is a clear choice put before all: For the wages of sin is death, but the gift of God is eternal life through Jesus our Lord. Sin is serious, either I pay the price of my own sin, or trust the substitute Saviour who died in my place. Sadly, many refuse and continue to sin, but *'Whoever calls upon the name of the Lord will be saved.'* (Romans 10:13).

∞

The Bible says, 'All we like sheep have gone astray; we have turned, every one, to his own way; and the Lord has laid on Him the iniquity of us all' ~ Isaiah 53:6

WHY
do Christians believe Jesus
rose from the dead?

T his is an old question. Speaking to a King in AD 59, Paul, the great missionary statesman, asked Agrippa, *'Why should it be though incredible to you that God raises the dead?'*

People constantly asked Jesus about life. If anyone knew about real life, Christ did. Ultimately His greatest demonstration of this was His resurrection from the dead.

Both secular and Christian history records that Jesus was cruelly beaten. He was scorned and spat upon, buffeted and bruised, crucified and killed. Roman executioners guaranteed that He was dead by thrusting a spear into Him and watching blood and water pour from His body. This body was to be embalmed, laid in an empty tomb and sealed in by a large boulder which was then guarded by soldiers. For three days His cold corpse lay there until the first Easter. Jesus rose and appeared to two women, two disciples, a couple walking, then ten of his disciples, and eventually to all including Thomas, who said he would not believe unless he could put his fingers in the wounds and his fist in His side. When he saw Jesus he knelt in awe and said, *'My Lord and my God.'* At one time Jesus appeared to a group of over five hundred people. He showed Himself in different places, at different times, and in different settings. He invited doubters to touch and see Him. Romans and Jesus would gladly have brought the body to the early Christians to silence their preaching about the risen Jesus. But they could not. He had certainly died, His body could not have been stolen; but the tomb was empty and many people actually saw, talked to and ate with the risen Christ. He transformed the disciples from timid, fearful followers, into bold witnesses of the death and resurrection of Christ who would die for the truth of what they had seen. Early Christians even changed their day of worship from Saturday to Sunday to commemorate His resurrection.

If people honestly question the resurrection they have to explain why the guarded tomb where the body of Jesus lay, was empty. Who was it who appeared to hundreds and convinced them that He was risen from the dead? Who changed the lives of the disappointed disciples, and who changes lives of those who turn from their sin, trusting the risen Saviour today? What Christ did in dying and rising from the dead was in fulfilment of both Old Testaments prophecy and His own words. It proves he is who he claimed to be; that He has power over sin and death, and that there is judgment and life after death.

∽

Dr. Frank Morrison, a London barrister, believed that the resurrection was only a fairytale happy ending. He wanted to write a book to disprove the resurrection once and for all. However, upon studying the facts, the sheer weight of evidence compelled him to conclude that Jesus actually rose from the dead. Frank Morrison wrote his book, but not the one he had planned. It is called, 'Who Moved The Stone?' The first chapter is called, 'The Book That Refused To Be Written'.

Paul the Apostle said, 'I declare to you the gospel ... that Christ died for our sins ... that He was buried, and that He rose again the third day according to the Scriptures'
~ I Corinthians 15:1-4

IF
Christ died for sin, why isn't everyone forgiven?

The cross of Christ really is central to the good news of the Lord Jesus. Christ was born to die. Hanging, suffering, bleeding and dying on the cross Jesus was paying the penalty of sin.

The cross is God's only means of forgiveness. Because Christ has died and risen there is a way of access to God, not only for life but for eternity,

> *There's a way back to God*
> *From the dark paths of sin;*
> *There's a door that is open,*
> *And you may go in:*
> *At Calvary's cross is where you begin,*
> *When you come as a sinner to Jesus.*

God offers to all pardon and peace, but offers no other route to Him and to heaven except through Christ.

If a person rejects or neglects Christ, then the responsibility of that choice is entirely his or hers. 'For the wages of sin is death, but the gift of God is eternal life in Christ Jesus our Lord.' (Romans 6:23). As with any other gift, it is first of all offered. Only those who repent, believe and accept the offered gift, can know the joy of having a clean and clear conscience before God.

'And if it seems evil to you to serve the Lord, choose yourselves this day whom you will serve, whether the gods which your fathers served that were on the other side of the River, or the gods of the Amorites, in whose land you dwell. But as for me and my house, we will serve the Lord' ~ Joshua 24:15

WHAT
happens to someone who commits suicide - do they go to hell?

To commit suicide is to break the sixth of the ten commandments, 'You shall not murder.' Because of some popular films which give the impression that suicide is a way of escape and a means of proving one's significance, suicide has been made to appear as one of a number of options when difficulties arise. There are well-known characters who have taken their own lives, and this has led to a knock-on effect of others imitating them.

Suicide is not a Christian response to difficulties. Characters in the Bible who asked God to take their lives from them, had their prayer refused, because the Lord had further work for them to do for Him and for others. When problems arise, I should not ask, 'How can I get out of this?' but 'What can I get out of this?'

There are some who have lost the balance of their minds and have consequently harmed themselves. But suicide is a selfish act, which leaves a wake of guilt and grief to those who are left behind.

However, the eternal destiny of men and women - heaven or hell - is dependant upon what that individual does with Jesus Christ. A person goes to heaven, because he or she has come to a moment in life when they have trusted Christ as Lord and Saviour, asking Christ to forgive all sin, and bring them into an everlasting relationship with God. A person will only go to hell because he or she has rejected God's love shown in the death and resurrection of the Lord Jesus Christ. That person has refused God's offer of new and everlasting life. It is possible that a genuine Christian, in an act of disobedience to God, or through mental disorder takes his or her own life. That is a great tragedy. However, it will not affect their place in heaven; that has been bought and reserved for them by Christ. God may not have called that Christian "home" to heaven at that time; but He will welcome them home nonetheless.

Somebody who is despairing, should turn to God and cry out to Him for help, and then seek the help of a godly pastor or friend, who can help them through the difficult times. Life is tough, but God is good.

Man is a prisoner who has no right to open the door of his prison and run away. A man should wait, and not take his own life until God summons him ~ Plato in 'Dialogues'

DOESN'T
Christianity take away my freedom?

Freedom to do as we choose isn't necessarily good. Should the drug pusher be free to peddle his wares regardless of the consequences? Should the murderer be allowed to continue killing? Should the joy rider be treated as having innocent fun? We know the correct answer to each of those questions. Liberty should not be a selfish licence. Real freedom is not doing as I please, but having the power to do what is right. Christianity is not rules and regulations. It is a living relationship with a loving God. Love God and do as you please. Love God, and you will find yourself living for Him and for others, and in so doing finding real pleasure which is illusive to so many who never turn to Him.

No man was ever so free as Jesus Christ. He could do all things. He was free from greed, free from sham and hypocrisy; he had no fear of what others might say or do to Him; in fact the Bible teaches that He deliberately 'made Himself of no reputation'. He was totally free to be Himself. He had a great sense of duty, but that did not thwart His personality. Obedience to His Father's will did not stifle Him. True freedom is found in Christ. He gives new desires, and the power to fulfil them. Jesus, who has said, 'I do always those things which please Him (God)' was the one who could then say, 'If the Son shall make you free, you will be free indeed.' In Christ, you start to become the person that God wants you to be, and then you can be free to be yourself.

❦

What is so notable about the twentieth century and a principal cause of its horrors is that great physical

power has been acquired by men who have no fear of God and who believe themselves restrained by no absolute code of conduct. ~ Dr. Paul Johnson, historian and journalist

The hope of the world is still in dedicated minorities. The trail blazers in human, academic, scientific and religious freedom have always been in the minority.
~ Martin Luther King

ISN'T
Christianity just a list of do's and don'ts?

Whe a couple marry, they agree to 'forsake all others' and live only with the chosen life-partner. There ought to be love and life and lasting pleasure in that relationship as it grows with passing years.

In a similar way, when a person enters by faith into a personal relationship with God through Christ, there will be a forsaking of all other claims on that life. Because Christians love their Lord, they will want to please Christ. There are certain places to which Christians will not go and certain things Christians will not do, simply because they would hurt the Christ who laid down His life to save them. The Christian has been bought with a price and therefore belongs to Christ.

The Christian life is not an easy one. It involves swimming against the tide of society. However, fullness of joy becomes the present experience of the person who is made right with God. Things that once seemed so appealing lose some of their attraction, because Christ and His Word become so precious. God by His Holy Spirit comes to live within the Christian, and He changes desires and delights. True pleasure is found in being the people we were created to be, in fellowship with God.

As a Christian, I have begun to experience the fullness of joy and do not need nor desire to chase around looking for quick-fix happiness. Christ satisfies those who know Him. Rather than rules and regulations, God's life in the heart of the Christian is based upon a living relationship with God Himself.

∽

Jesus said, 'If anyone desires to come after me, let him deny himself, and take up his cross daily, and follow me.'
~ Luke 9:23

HOW
will the world end?

The Bible makes it clear that the world will not come to an end by a nuclear bomb, or a collision with another planet, but God will bring to an end the world's system in His time.

Jesus Christ will return to this earth, not as a baby to be laid in a manger, but as the King of kings and Lord of lords. Nobody knows the day nor the hour when this will happen, but Jesus described how the world will be immediately before His return, in Matthew chapter twenty-four. He said to His disciples that just as He was to leave the earth to prepare a place in heaven for them, so He would return to earth again to receive them to Himself.

The Bible describes what will happen when He returns: *'For this we say to you by the word of the Lord, that we who are alive and remain until the coming of the Lord will by no means precede those who are asleep. For the Lord Himself will descend from heaven with a shout, with the voice of an archangel, and with the trumpet of God. And the dead in Christ will arise first. Then we who are alive and remain shall be caught up together with them in the clouds to meet the Lord in the air, and thus we shall always be with the Lord.'* (I Thessalonians 4:15-17).

Every true Christian looks forward to the bodily return of Jesus Christ. It seems that so many of the signs which will come to pass just before His return have indeed happened. When he comes He will divide those who are not trusting Him from those who are.

The most vital questions for you are, *'Are you ready for the return of Jesus Christ?'* *'Is He your Lord and Saviour now?'*

Jesus said, 'For whoever is ashamed of me and my words, of him the Son of Man will be ashamed when He comes in His own glory, and in His Father's, and in the glory of the holy angels' ~ Luke 9:26

WHY
are there so many types
of Churches?

C hurches are to do with people. All who are truly in Christ and wanting to follow Him will want to meet together to worship, pray, praise, hear God's Word preached, enjoy fellowship and serve God.

Sadly, almost from the beginning of Christianity, people have drifted from simply accepting what the Bible says. Often morality or politics has become the message instead of the living truth found in God's Word. There is nothing more dull and dismal than religious rites and ritual without the reality and vitality of knowing a living relationship with God. When groups have gone like this, in time God has raised up others who establish a church or Christian gathering of people who love the Lord and His Word, and who simply want to meet with others who seek to put God first in their lives.

Look for a Church which really does love the Lord Jesus and seeks to follow Him.

Such a group will pray and study the Bible together. They will believe the historic Christian Gospel, and will do their utmost to share Christ with others.

Churches like this are far from boring, but will be caring, enthusiastic and growing - their joy and love is infectious. However, you will never find the perfect church.

If you were looking for a gathering of whole and healthy people you would not go to a hospital. A church is a gathering of sinners - if they have trusted Christ, they are forgiven sinners. Nevertheless, until heaven, nothing on earth, even the church, is perfect. Despite this, all who know and love the Lord Jesus will want to meet with other believers to worship, work and witness together. Jesus set the example of worship. We read, *'So He came to Nazareth where He had been brought up. And as His custom was, He went into the synagogue on the Sabbath day, and stood up to read'* Luke 4:16

❧

CH_ _CH - What is missing?
UR!

WHY
are there scandals in the Church?

Sadly, sometimes things do go wrong in the church. This is always a grief to real Christian people. But then Christians are only people - ordinary sinners, who have asked Christ to forgive them and to be Lord of their lives. A Christian is not perfect, only forgiven! The church is rather like a hospital, a centre for all sorts of needs, and it is therefore inevitable that things will go wrong. Nevertheless, that is no excuse, and every Christian will sincerely want to live in a way which is pleasing to God and to others. This will apply at home, at work, in leisure and in the church.

A truly Bible-believing church, where Christ is honoured and loved can be a wonderful haven of fellowship, peace and encouragement. It is a place of real blessing enjoyed by so many. Going to church in itself does not make a person a Christian, but I recommend getting involved in an evangelical church of whichever denomination suits you and is nearest you. You will not regret it.

✿

The Christian church is the only society in the world in which membership is based upon the qualification that the candidate shall be unworthy of membership.
~ Charles C. Morrison

ISN'T

the Church one of the world's richest organisations?

hrist did not come to earth to establish a wealthy, bureaucratic organisation! He Himself had nothing - He preached from a borrowed boat, borrowed a coin to illustrate a simple point, rode to Jerusalem on a borrowed donkey and was buried in a borrowed tomb. He said, speaking of Himself, 'Foxes have holes, birds of the air have their nests, but the Son of Man has nowhere to lay His head.'

The early church did not accumulate money. Peter said to a lame man, 'Silver and gold I do not have, but what I do have I give you: In the name of Jesus Christ of Nazareth, rise up and walk."

If certain churches have gathered to themselves great wealth, it is a sign that they have moved away from the Bible's teaching that the things that God gives us are to be used for the blessing and benefit of others. There are many examples of Christian people, organisations and churches who have wholeheartedly used the resources that they have to meet the needs of others throughout the world, who are less fortunate than themselves. Quiet, self-sacrificing service is the hall-mark of much Christian activity.

❧

Oliver Cromwell, speaking of silver and gold statues in churches said, 'Melt down the saints and put them into circulation!'

HOW
can I get right with God?

There are Christians on all continents and countries, of all ages and of every status in life. God commands all people everywhere to repent (that is turn from sin), and to believe (that is to trust in Christ). As a person does this, he or she will discover that God has turned to them to cleanse them from every sin, come into their lives and become their Companion for ever. A Christian, therefore, has trusted the crucified Christ as Saviour, and the risen Christ as Lord.

Will you now, in a definite and deliberate act, confess your sin to God,
come to Him for forgiveness and new life,
commit yourself to Him,
crown Him as your Lord and Saviour?

God will not only cast all your sins behind His back and remember them no more, but He will become your Friend, never to leave you or forsake you. He will be with you in life, in death and throughout eternity.

❧

Jesus, 'The one who comes to me I will by no means cast out.' ~ John 6:37

WHY

should the Christian Church be the right one? Aren't all the other ideas about God just as valid?

The true and living God has revealed Himself to this world, so that we are able to find out about Him, and so discover what He is like. By looking at the person of Jesus Christ and by reading the Bible, we can discover the living and the written word of God. He has shown Himself to be a holy God who has provided a way whereby people who have done wrong can find forgiveness and spiritual life through Christ.

Only Christ lived a pure and sinless life which qualified Him to be able to die for the sins of the world. Only He had power over nature, disease, the devil and death. Only He could rise from the dead having taken on Himself the sin of the world and paid for it.

> *There was no other good enough*
> *To pay the price of sin*
> *He only could unlock the gates of heaven*
> *And let us in.*

❧

When I discuss the spiritual issue with my overseas colleagues, several of whom are Moslems and Hindus, I ask them two questions: 'Do you know your sins are forgiven?' and 'Do you know you are going to heaven when you die?' Their usual answer is, 'I hope so'. But there is no certainty because there is no righteous basis on which their god can be just and justify the guilty sinner.
- Professor Verna Wright, Leeds University

ISN'T
Christianity just a crutch for the weak?

If I break a leg, I would not mind using a crutch. If I am sick, I do not mind going to a doctor. As I have sinned and guilt is a reality, I need someone who can forgive me. If that 'crutch' is the Lord Jesus, who has proved clearly that for centuries He is able to make thieves... honest; drunkards... sober; immoral people... pure; blasphemers... kind in their talk; the weak... strong and the godless people... godly; then surely He is worth resting on and receiving the peace, pardon and purpose which He offers!

❦

'Casting all your care upon Him, for He cares for you'
~ I Peter 5:7

WHAT

about the people who have never heard the Christian message? Where do they go?

There is only one way to God and that is through Jesus Christ. He said, "I am the way, the truth and the life; no one comes to the Father but through Me." (John 14 v. 6). There are people in the world who have never heard the gospel, and we trust God, our loving Creator to be fair and just. The Judge of all the earth will do right. We know that Christ came into the world not to condemn the world, but that the world through Him might be saved (John 3 v. 17). Those who go to hell do so because they have rejected God's means of forgiveness.

There is sufficient evidence in creation itself to know that there is a God of order and love. There is within everyone a sense of right and wrong, and an awareness that there is a God. People have to suppress this before they can deny His existence. Those who know no more than that will be judged fairly according to the light that they have received. Perhaps they will be judged in a different court room, so to speak. We who have had opportunity to repent and believe will be judged as to what we have done with Christ.

❧

In God is my salvation and my glory; the rock of my strength, and my refuge, is in God. Trust in Him at all times, you people; pour out your heart to Him; God is a refuge for us ... Power belongs to God. Also to You, O Lord, belongs mercy; for You render to each one according to his work.
~ Psalm 62 v. 7, 8, 11 & 12

HOW
should a Christian live?

The moment a person receives Christ as Lord and Saviour, he or she enters into a wonderful relationship with the true and living God. This needs to be cultivated and deepened. Therefore, it is vital to spend time with the Lord and the Lord's people. If a Christian is to grow in the knowledge of Jesus Christ it is important to find a good, Bible-believing church where there is real love, care and good Bible teaching; and where one can start to be involved using one's talents for God's glory.

Spending time daily, systematically reading a portion of the Bible and praying is a key part of the Christian's life. God will teach the Bible-reader and give a clearer understanding of His will for life. Praying is speaking to God. It involves worshipping Him, confessing sin, claiming new forgiveness and praying for the needs of others and one's self.

A Christian will want to share the Gospel. Christians should not be secret disciples, but should make it a constant aim to introduce others to Christ, both by speaking about and living for Christ.

A Christian should keep trusting the Lord Jesus, the living Saviour, in times of joy or temptation, doubt of difficulty. He is a constant companion. If we ask Him, He will take us through every situation.

The Christian life is an exciting one, because the God of all creation comes to guide and guard in a very personal way. The Christian's life is in His hands. His love is utterly consistent and He will never fail.

Remember, He takes a person as a sinner, and a Christian will never be a disappointment to Him! Step by step God will work in a believer to make him or her more like Himself.

❧

God says, 'Fear not, for I am with you; be not dismayed, for I am your God. I will strengthen you, yes, I will help you, I will uphold you with my righteous right hand.' ~ Isaiah 41:10

WHO
is Jesus Christ?

The Bible makes it very clear that there is only one God. This one God is in three persons - God the Father, the Son and the Holy Spirit.

God clothed Himself in humanity in the person of Jesus Christ. God became man and dwelt among us. The Bible puts it this way:

'For unto us a child is born, unto us a Son is given; and the government will be upon his shoulder. And His name will be called Wonderful, Counsellor, Mighty God, Everlasting Father, Prince of Peace.' (Isaiah 9:6).

'In the beginning was the Word, and the Word was with God, and the Word was God.' (John 1:1).

'And the Word became flesh and dwelt among us, and we beheld His glory, the glory as of the only begotten of the Father, full of grace and truth.' (John 1:14).

Here is a story which actually happened on the evening of a school nativity play. Old folk and parents had gathered in the school hall. Everything was going well until the wise men appeared all dressed up. When the third one saw his parents in the audience, his mouth fell open and he forgot his words. He was overawed.

Slowly the boy knelt by the manger to present his gift and say his lines, but no words came.

The teacher in the wings whispered, *'Say something.'*

No words came, *'Say anything,'* the teacher said in desperation.

'Eeh, he's just like his dad!' the young actor said.

How right he was. The baby born in Bethlehem was the express image of His Father God. The Creator had become like us, His creation. God had become a man.

"God was in Christ reconciling the world to Himself, not imputing their trespasses to them, and has committed us to the word of reconciliation.' (2 Corinthians 5:19).

Jesus came into the world to save His people from their sins. Because He cared He gave sight to the blind, hearing to the deaf, speech to the dumb, strength to the lame, cleansing to the leprous, life to the dead, food to the hungry, peace to the troubled, comfort to the grieving and forgiveness to the guilty.

He had come to die. In dying He was bearing in His own body the sin of the world. In rising from the dead He conquered the great conqueror, death. He came from God that He might bring us to God. Christ is not only the greatest human who ever lived, who gave to the world the greatest teaching ever given, but He is the Creator, stepping into the areas of human history to rescue men and women from sin and bring them back to God.

∽

**'God was manifested in the flesh,
Justified in the Spirit,
Seen by angels,
Preached among the Gentiles,
Believed on in the world,
Received up in glory'
~ I Timothy 3:16**

As the person of Jesus Christ has been attacked by various sects, here is a shortened list of some Bible references which give verses to demonstrate that Jesus is God manifest in the flesh.

Matthew 1:23; Mark 5:6-7; John 1:1, 2, 14; John 5:17, 18, 21-23; John 10:30-33; John 20:28; Acts 20:28; Romans 9:5; Philippians 2:6; I Timothy 3:16; Titus 2:13; Hebrews 1:8-10.

WHAT
good has Christ done for the world?

Jesus Christ is the greatest man of history. He came not to call righteous people to Himself, but sinners. When such people turn from their sins in repentance and trust Christ by faith, He completely changes their lives. These transformed people have received a desire and a power to change their world. Many of Britain's social reforms were brought about through Christ changing lives: William Wilberforce worked for the abolition of slavery, after he was converted to Christ; Elizabeth Fry and John Howard worked for prison reform because of their love for Christ; Lord Shaftesbury, a committed Christian, worked for the poor, changing laws governing work in factories and for children; Dr. Barnardo, George Muller and Thomas Stephenson showed God's love for individuals by housing orphans; Florence Nightingale cared for wounded soldiers because she was grateful to God for His love for her.

Our educational system is indebted to Christians for its origin, as are hospitals and many welfare institutions. Even trade unions had their beginnings in Methodism, as did the Labour Party.

Christ gave dignity to women, respect to the disabled, significance to children, credibility to the family, and status to each individual. We owe our democratic freedoms to people who laid down their lives so that we might have freedom of conscience in the land. Christ has made an indelible impact upon our literature, art, music and architecture.

As missionaries have taken the good news of Jesus Christ throughout the world, people who have been held in the grip of pagan darkness have been liberated and given new joys in living, and peace with God, as well as with themselves and with others.

Many of the world's greatest scientists have been people who have trusted in God and believed in the person of Christ. They have laboured to discover the workings of nature, believing that God is reliable, and a God of order. Examples include: Leonardo da Vinci, Johann Kepler, Francis Bacon, Blaise Pascal, Robert Boyle, Nicholas Copernicus, Isaac Newton, Michael Faraday, Humphrey Davy, Samuel Morse, Louis Agassiz, Louis Pasteur and George Washington Carver.

Primarily, He has forgiven millions of people who have simply trusted Him as their personal Lord and Saviour. He has given joy, peace, power and love to those who have come to know Him in a personal way. He has been a guide and friend to all types as they have faced the joys and difficulties of life. He has been with them as they have died, and he has taken them to be with Him in heaven.

❧

Amazing grace!
How sweet the sound
That saved a wretch like me -
I once was lost, but now am found;
Was blind but now I see.
~ John Newton, converted slave-trader

WHY
do Christians believe what
they do about sex?

God created sex. It is a good gift from a good God. He made the desire for the opposite sex which is part of us all. That is natural, but exploited.

God is our Maker. Following the manufacturer's instructions is always the best rule. Today's pressure says, 'If it feels good, do it.' This may be tempting, but God because of His love for us has designated something better.

The Bible says, *'For this reason a man shall leave his father and mother and be joined to his wife, and the two shall become one flesh.'* (Ephesians 5:31). Sexual intercourse between a husband and wife is to be a mutual expression of love within a wholesome and secure relationship.

Sex outside the mutual commitment of marriage is not what God designed. Where there is sex before marriage there will not be trust within marriage, and without mutual trust there cannot be the depth of a relationship in which marriage delights.

God's pattern is that two people should be drawn towards each other until it is right and they are ready to commit and submit themselves to their life-partner. The couple have slowly become one in mind, heart and outlook, and so it is natural that they become one in body too. There is nothing dirty or smutty about sex when experienced in this way. Rather it is God's wedding present to the married couple. It is a gift which shall last until death parts them.

It is typical of the world though, that we try to cheat God and corrupt the purity of sex. In whatever way this is done - sex before marriage, adultery, homosexuality, watching dirty videos or TV programmes, reading smutty magazines or newspapers, it leads to unhappiness. One of the joys of marriage is sex without guilt.

To some extent we all fail. When Christ died He took on Himself all sin, including that of moral failure. He has paid the price of our wrong doing. *'The blood of Jesus Christ, God's Son cleanses us from all sin.'* (1 John 1:7). *'If we confess our sins (to God), He is faithful and just to forgive us our sins and to cleanse us from all unrighteousness.'* (1 John 1:9).

Ask Christ for cleansing from sin and the power to live and do right. He will give it to those who sincerely seek Him.

∽

'Therefore if the Son makes you free, you shall be free indeed.' ~ John 8:36

WHAT
is wrong with homosexuality?

God the Maker created men and women to be physically and temperamentally different so that there would be balance and completion in the male/female relationship.

Christianity is not against homosexuals as people. God cares for and deeply loves all His creation. But homosexuality itself goes against nature. God-designated sexuality is to be expressed between a husband and wife within the form and freedom of a married relationship. Marital sex is an expression of love and the means for human reproduction. It is as well that homosexuals' parents were not homosexual! There may be many reasons why a person becomes homosexual, not all the fault of the person concerned. Nevertheless the Bible teaches that to practise homosexuality is sin, but that God is able to forgive that and all other sins. (See Romans chapter one).

There is a book in the Bible written to a group of Christians who had led grossly ungodly lives before coming to trust Christ. This is how Paul wrote to them.

'Do you not know that the unrighteous will not inherit the kingdom of God? Do not be deceived. Neither fornicators, nor idolaters, nor adulterers, nor homosexuals, nor sodomites, nor thieves, nor covetous, nor drunkards, nor revilers, nor extortioners will inherit the kingdom of God. And such were some of you. But you were washed, but you were sanctified, but you were justified in the name of the Lord Jesus and by the Spirit of our God. " (1 Corinthians 6:9-11).

Not only were these people forgiven but they were changed by the power of God. The Bible says, *'He who covers his sins will not prosper, but whoever confesses and forsakes them will have mercy'* (Proverbs 28:13).

That mercy can bring a person to God and change the very desire of the person who trusts Christ as Lord and Saviour.

❧

'And the Lord caused a deep sleep to fall on Adam, and he slept; and He took one of his ribs, and closed up the flesh in its place. Then the rib which the Lord God had taken from man He made into woman, and He brought her to the man.'
'And Adam said, This is now bone of my bone and flesh of my flesh; she shall be called Woman, because she was taken out of man.'
'Therefore a man shall leave his father and mother and be joined to his wife, and they shall become one flesh.'
~ From Genesis chapter two

IS
the mass media and the pop scene against Christianity?

We are living in a society which has basically turned its back on God. It is not so much that people cannot believe but that they do not want to. Whilst the mass media pays a nodding respect to religion on Sunday mornings, there usually is constant subtle undermining of all things to do with the Lord and the Bible. It is good to be aware of this. Frankly, people who spend their time taking in the views of the mass media are allowing themselves to be brainwashed. The Bible teaches that whoever has control over his mind is greater than the one who captures a city. We must all be careful to ensure that the things that fill our minds are true, noble, just, pure, lovely, of good report, virtuous and praiseworthy. Philippians 4:8.

Before imbibing cynical and godless comments from presenters, actors, entertainers or writers, it is a good thing to consider their life styles. Are their family lives strong? Are they moral people? Is their language clean? The Bible teaches that when people shamelessly live for idolatry or immorality and don't like to keep God in their knowledge, God gives them up. These are not the people to make heroes of or to be influenced by. One day God will judge all according to what each has done with the Lord Jesus. Until then, while we have life, the most important thing is to come to know the true and living God and live for and with Him.

❧

'What is still called Western civilisation is an advanced stage of decomposition.' ~ Malcolm Muggeridge

WHAT
do you think of the National Lottery?

mbition is a motivation which can drive a person to the pursuit of excellence, and that cannot be wrong. However, greed is based upon discontent, and the mistaken belief that having more will bring happiness.

The tenth commandment states, 'You shall not covet …' That means that we are not to be enviously longing for the things that others have, but to be content with what God has given us. 'Godliness with contentment is great gain.' The lottery exploits a deep and unhealthy longing for more. Despite the evidence that vast wins wreck the lives of the winners, there is a feeling in the heart of the gambler, that he or she would be an exception to that rule.

When Christ was being crucified, taking on Himself the sins of the world, a group of soldiers were at the foot of the cross, gambling for His garments. It was an insult to the God of the commandments who is the God of the cross.

⁓

Mae West was asked which she would choose if she had the choice between winning $10,000,000 or having ten children. She replied that she would have the children. When asked why, she replied, 'Because if I had ten children, I wouldn't want any more!'

WHY
go to Church on Sunday?
Isn't it just another day?

When God had created the world, He rested in victory on 'the Sabbath'. For faithful Jews it was to remind them of God, and His work of creation. The fourth commandment says, 'Remember the Sabbath day to keep it holy ...'

Jesus, having been crucified and buried, rose again on the first day of the week, the day after the Jewish Sabbath, namely Sunday. Early Christians began to worship together on Sunday to remember the Lord Jesus and His work of re-creation. Exactly seven weeks after the resurrection of Christ, the Holy Spirit descended to dwell in the hearts and lives of Christian people. This happened at Pentecost, so Christians also remember the work of the Holy Spirit and His work of procreation.

It is a day set aside for God and worship. Individuals and nations are blessed in keeping the day as sacred. Personally, I do not shop or do unnecessary work on Sunday. I try not to cause work for others on that day. I have benefited tremendously by seeking to keep 'the Lord's Day' (as the Bible calls it) as a holy day. I start the week with the first day being given to God, and I find He amply rewards that practice.

❧

The film 'Chariots of Fire' reminded the world of Eric Liddell. He was the Scottish Olympic athlete who refused to run in the 100 metres on a Sunday. The reason was that Eric was a Christian. Eric believed the Bible's teaching that God will honour those who honour Him. A few days after his scheduled race, Eric ran, won and set a new world record for the 400 metres in the Paris Olympics of 1924. He said, 'I believe that Sunday as we have had it in the past, is one of the greatest helps in a young man's life to keep all that is noblest, truest and best.'

CAN
you be a Christian and not go to Church?

This question is rather like asking, *'Can you be married and not live together?'* The answer, of course, is *'Yes'* but there is something wrong with a marriage which is in such a state.

A Christian is someone who has turned from his or her sin (repentance) to put his or her faith in Christ who died for sin and rose again as conqueror over sin, death and the devil. Christ is both Lord and Saviour of a real Christian.

When someone truly trusts Christ, God gives spiritual life. Many things are changed when a person is converted, but basically the Christian has a relationship with God that is real and deep. A real believer will want to meet with others who trust Christ. Christians are great to be with because of their love for the Lord, as well as their genuine and growing concern for others.

Christian worship is exhilarating if it comes from the heart of a people who are thrilled by God Himself and all that He has done. To listen to somebody who loves Christ, teaching the Bible to those who are keen to grow in their knowledge of God, is not dry or boring but exciting. The Bible teaches that God inhabits the praises of His people. To be in a place where God is loved and honoured is a delight and joy to a real Christian. If you do not experience this, perhaps there is something wrong with your church, or may be you have never really trusted Christ as Saviour and Lord.

Question: Can I be a Christian without joining the church?

Answer: Yes, it is possible. It is something like being a student who will not go to school, a soldier who will not join an army, a citizen who does not pay taxes or vote, a salesman with no customers, an explorer with no base camp, a seaman on a ship without a crew, a businessman on a desert island, an author without readers, a tuba player without an orchestra, a parent without a family, a football player without a team, a politician who is a hermit, a scientist who does not share his findings, a bee without a hive.

DON'T
you find Churches are full of hypocrites?

Going to church does not make a person a Christian. It is well known that the lives of some churchgoers have proved to be a sham, and they have brought shame on themselves and the name of the Lord. It has always been like that.

Nevertheless, abuse of Christ does not mean that He is not real. Millions have found Him to be the precious Saviour who totally changes all who come to Him with sincerity and faith.

Outside a respectable Anglican Church in Yorkshire the vicar hung a banner saying, 'Only sinners welcome here!' It caused some offence, but he was right. Whether the sin is hypocrisy or some other wrong attitude or action, all need the Saviour and all are welcome to respond to Christ's invitation to *'Come unto Me, all you who labour and are heavy laden, and I will give you rest.'* (Matthew 11:28).

Remember, if you find fault with those professing real Christian faith, they are only sinners who have found the Saviour whom we all need. As they continue in their Christian life, Christ will refine their character so that they will gradually become more and more the people He wants them to be.

❧

Don't stay away from church because there are so many hypocrites; there is always room for one more.

ISN'T
faith a leap in the dark?

Blind faith is a leap in the dark, but that is folly. Christian faith is resting on the promises of God. It is based upon the solid foundation of God's Word the Bible, and God's work in the world and through His Son Jesus. The faith that saves a person is not whimsical or mystical. It relies on the solid historical truth of the life, death and resurrection of Jesus.

Faith is a gift from God; He will give it to those who seek. In the Bible we read, *'So then faith comes by hearing, and hearing by the Word of God'*. (Romans 10:17). When a person reads the Bible with an open heart, God creates faith, He speaks to that individual concerning the truth of what is being written.

The Gospel of John is a good place to begin. Towards the end of that Gospel we read John's motive for writing it, *'And truly Jesus did many other signs in the presence of His disciples, which are not written in this book; but these are written that you may believe that Jesus is the Christ, the Son of God and that believing you may have life in His name.'* (John 20:30, 31).

Christianity stands up to the test of cross-examination. Historically, archaeologically, scientifically, logically and experientially it is accurate. Faith is the act of committing one's self to Christ on the basis of the truth of all that God has revealed. Then, when spiritual life follows, that faith becomes even more sure and certain.

Faith is one of the most precious treasures a man can possibly possess. It is a pity that so few understand what the Bible teaches about it. Faith is often confused with presumption, optimism, determination, superstition and imagination. Actually, it is simply believing ... obviously faith honours God, while doubting His Word must insult and displease Him. ~ Weekly Review

DO YOU
believe Jesus was born of a virgin?

If God stepped into time and space as a man who was as the Bible teaches, fully man and fully God, then He would have to have been born both of a human being and of God.

Mary, the mother of Jesus was committed to be married to Joseph. They had not had sexual relations. God miraculously worked in Mary so that she conceived and gave birth to the baby Jesus.

This had been foretold 700 years before by the prophet Isaiah, *'Behold a virgin shall be with child, and bear a son, and they shall call His name 'Immanuel' which is being translated 'God with us''* (Isaiah 7:14 and Matthew 1:23). It is described as a special sign in Isaiah - a young woman bearing a child in the normal way is hardly a special sign of the birth of the Messiah!

Mary was perplexed and asked how she could be pregnant since she had not 'known' a man. When Joseph heard that Mary was expecting a child he feared the worst concerning his fiancée, but God reassured Mary, and later Joseph, saying, *'That which is conceived in her is of the Holy Spirit, and she will bring forth a Son and you shall call His name Jesus, for He will save His people from their sins.'* (Matthew 1:20, 21).

It is clear from the Bible that later Mary and Joseph were married and were to have children through natural conception. (Matthew 13:55, 56). At least one of these brothers, James, was to become a convinced follower of the Lord Jesus Christ after His resurrection.

Napoleon said, 'I know men; and I tell you that Jesus Christ is not a man. Superficial minds see a resemblance between Christ and the founders of empires, and the gods of other religions. That resemblance does not exist. There is between Christianity, and whatever other religions, the distance of infinity ... Everything in Christ astonishes me. His spirit overawes me, and His will confounds me. Between Him and whoever else in the world, there is no possible term of comparison. He is truly a being by Himself.

His ideas and sentiments, and the truth which He announces, His manner of convincing, are not explained either by human organisation or by the nature of things ... The nearer I approach, the more carefully I examine, everything is above me - everything remains grand, of a grandeur which overpowers. His religion is a revelation from an intelligence which certainly is not of man ... One can absolutely find nowhere, but in Him alone, the initiation of the example of His life ... I search in vain in history to find the similar to Jesus Christ, or anything which can approach the gospel.'

WHAT
exactly does it mean to be converted?

C hrist did not come into the world to call the righteous, but to save sinners. Jesus said that each individual needs to have a total life and eternity changing experience where one finds forgiveness for sin and faith in the Saviour. He said to a religious teacher called Nicodemus, *'Most assuredly, I say to you, unless one is born again, he cannot see the kingdom of God.'* John 3:3. Jesus also said, *'Assuredly, I say to you, unless you are converted and become as little children, you will by no means enter the kingdom of heaven.'* (Matthew 18:3). Have you been converted?

Three things happen when you are converted to Christ:

1. There is an act of will as you turn from your sin. This is not an emotion or feeling but a deliberate willingness to turn away from all sinful practices and habits. God will give you the strength to do so if you are willing.

2. There is an act of the mind and heart as you turn to Christ. Christ carried on the cross all our public and private sins; the sins we regret and remember as well as those we relish and run to. We need to trust Christ to take away our sins and live within us as our Companion and Friend.

3. There is an act of God as He turns to you. In the moment you ask Christ to be your Lord and Saviour, you will find that God has worked a miracle within you. He brings you into a friendship with Himself. You become God's and God becomes yours, forever. This is true Christian conversion. The famous

evangelist DL Moody said, *'If I can get a man to think for five minutes about his soul, he is almost certain to be converted.'* Conversion is a miracle, but it is wonderful. It can happen to you.

∽

In his autobiography, Col. Harland Sanders of Kentucky Friend Chicken fame says that he was always a God-fearing man. In every venture he gave God a tenth of the profits, yet he knew that if he died, God probably wouldn't take him to heaven. Worried, he travelled to Australia to a special church convention for the answer. He didn't find it. One day, Sanders was walking down a street in Louisville, Kentucky, when there the Rev. Waymon Rodgers of Louisville's Evangel Tabernacle invited him to some evangelistic services. Several days later Sanders went. At age 79 he claimed the promises of Romans 10:9: 'That if you confess with your mouth the Lord Jesus and believe in your heart that God has raised Him from the dead, you will be saved.' 'When I walked out of that church that night, I knew I was a different man. All my tithing and good deeds had never given me the sense of God's presence that I knew then,' he says.

CAN
I repent on my death bed?

The good news of Jesus Christ is so great that a godless person dying can still come to faith in Christ and find forgiveness. *'Whosoever calls on the name of the Lord shall be saved,'* the Bible says.

When Christ was on the cross, two thieves were crucified with him. One, hours away from death and meeting his Maker, was promised paradise.

Luke 23:39-43 tells us the story:

'Then one of the criminals who were hanged blasphemed him saying, 'If you are the Christ, save yourself and us.' But the other, answering, rebuked him saying, "Do you not even fear God, seeing you are under the same condemnation? And we indeed justly, for we receive the due reward of our deeds; but this man has done nothing wrong.'

'Then he said to Jesus, 'Lord, remember me when you come into your kingdom.' And Jesus said to him, 'Assuredly, I say to you, today you will be with me in paradise.'

There were four stages in the thoughts of the thief who trusted Christ:

First, his thoughts were of God; secondly, he saw his sin; thirdly, he considered Christ and fourthly he put his trust in Christ. Christ was bearing his sin on Himself on the cross. That is why Christ could say, *'Today you will be with me in paradise.'* In his dying moments the thief who was being executed for his crimes and deserved hell, found faith and forgiveness in Christ.

However, God does not promise a death bed. He does not even guarantee tomorrow. You could die in your sleep or in an accident. Now is the day to be saved. Those who hope to repent at the eleventh hour often die at 10:30pm.

My experience in visiting hospices is that those who have neglected getting right with God whilst fit and well, rarely want to sort things out spiritually when they are dying.

One other thought: repentance is being sorry for sin and not just for self. If God is God, serve Him. Make Him Lord of your life and live in a right relationship with Him. Don't just give him the 'fag end' of your life.

∽

'Deathbed repentance is burning the candle of life in the service of the devil and then blowing the smoke into the face of God.' ~ US preacher, Billy Sunday

'No man ever repented on his deathbed of being a Christian.' ~ Homah Moore

HOW
do I actually become a Christian?

Nobody is born a Christian. Going to church, trying hard, doing your best, becoming a church member, being baptised or confirmed does not make you a Christian. There has to come a moment of Christian conversion when turning from your own ways you commit yourself to Jesus Christ.

The Bible says, *'But as many as received Him to them he gave the right to become children of God, even to those who believe in His name.'* *'Believing in'* is an act of trust and faith. If I go to hospital for an operation, I have to believe in the anaesthetist and surgeon, as I put myself totally in their care and control. If I get on a plane I believe in the pilot to guide and direct the plane and me to the correct destination. Believing in Christ is putting my trust in Him to forgive and save me.

> *Upon a life I did not live,*
> *Upon a death I did not die,*
> *Upon Another's life,*
> *Another's death,*
> *I stake my whole eternity.*

Many have found that praying with similar words to the ones below has helped them to put their trust in Christ:

'Dear God, I want to confess my sin to you and in repentance turn from it. I believe that Jesus Christ died on the cross for my sin. I believe He rose from the dead. Please, forgive me and come to live in my life. Help me to live for You day by day.

Thank you for hearing this prayer which I pray in Jesus' name. Amen'

If you can pray such a prayer meaning every word, then pray it aloud to God who hears, promises to answer, and will make you His forever.

∽

Augustine prayed, 'Lord, save me from all my sins, but not yet.' There was no answer. Later he prayed, 'Lord, save me from my sins, except one.' Still there was no answer. Finally he prayed, 'Lord, save me from all my sins, and save me now!' God answered instantly!

IF I
become a Christian how could I keep up with that lifestyle?

The Christian life is all to do with Christ. He goes before, beside and behind the person who trusts Him.

He never leaves nor forsakes the one who has become a son or a daughter of God. He gives the strength and ability to do what is right and be the people He wants us to be. *'For me to live is Christ,'* said Paul the great Christian pioneer of early church history.

A Christian is well aware that he or she is not always the person that God would want, but the forgiveness which Christ purchased on the cross was for all sin - past, present and future.

The Christian life is an endless series of new beginnings. We should never contemplate the possibility of sin, but *'if anyone sins, we have an Advocate with the Father, Jesus Christ the righteous."* (John 2:1). Do not expect sin, excite sin or excuse sin.

Christ who lives in the Christian by His Holy Spirit will keep me saved, sure and satisfied throughout my Christian life's journey. As I trust and obey Him, He gives real and lasting joy.

~

'When a person is converted he is not only forgiven, he becomes a member of God's family. He is a child of God. The family likeness should soon begin to show. The family privileges are immediately his. He can pray to his Heavenly Father, who listens, plans, guides, protects and provides for his every need.' ~ Trevor Knight, Director, Young Life

WHY
don't miracles happen today?

They do! God answers prayer. It is a delightful habit of my life to spend time each day with God. In that time, I read some of the Bible, and in so doing God teaches me, and I pray. Time and time again I have found that God has wonderfully answered my prayers. What some would say are merely 'coincidences' happen when I pray, but do not occur if I am not praying. God's timing of events, providing of things, and dealings with me are miracles.

The greatest miracle for me was when I actually trusted Christ and asked Him to live in my heart and life. How He changed me!

Since then I have met people whose lives were completely changed too. Drunks were made sober; thieves were made honest; immoral people were made pure; blasphemers spoke kindly words.

I recently received this letter from a prisoner who had not long since become a Christian:- *'As the jury pronounced me 'Guilty', and the judge sentenced me, I felt God pronounced me 'Forgiven, on all accounts, through the blood of Jesus Christ.'*

What is this if it is not a miracle? Christ is not a psychological prop but the miracle working God who can change you today if you trust Him. When you do, even the miraculous provision of sun, rain, food, flowers, beauty and kindness become something to be grateful for rather than being taken for granted.

❧

'Some of the scribes and Pharisees asked, 'Teacher, we want to see a sign from You.' But He answered and said unto

them, 'An evil and adulterous generation seeks after a sign and no sign will be given to it except the sign of the prophet Jonah. For as Jonah was three days and three nights in the belly of the great fish, so will the Son of Man be three days and three nights in the heart of the earth.'
~ Matthew 12:38-40

MY
question to you

All of these questions have been asked in different ways time and time again by inquisitive minds.

Of necessity, the answers have been brief outlines rather than thorough arguments. As we come to the end of this book, permit me to ask you, the reader, one question:

What will you do with Jesus Christ?

The Bible says: *'Choose for yourselves this day whom you will serve.'*(Joshua 24:15). You can either reject or receive Him; turn away or turn to Him. Christ is able and willing to cleanse you from every sin as He comes to live within you.

Your response will affect your life, death and eternity.

With all sincerity, I would urge you to take steps to find peace with God.

Look again at the questions and answers about becoming a Christian and receive Christ as your Lord and Saviour today.

There's a way back to God
From the dark paths of sin,
There's a door that is open
And you may go in,
At Calvary's cross is where you begin
When you come as a sinner to Jesus.

At Easter time 1988, British stamps were franked by the post office with the words, 'Jesus Is Alive'. That is absolutely true, and it is a first class message! There is life after death, and both heaven and hell are taught in the Bible. Christ died to remove the sin that otherwise would keep you from heaven. Eternity depends on what you will do with Jesus Christ. The verdict is yours. What will you do with Jesus? One day you may be asking, 'What will He do with me?'